FABRIC ART

John Lancaster

Consultant: Henry Pluckrose

Photography: Chris Fairclough

FRANKLIN WATTS
New York/London/Sydney/Toronto

Copyright © 1990 Franklin Watts

Franklin Watts Inc
387 Park Avenue South
New York
NY 10016

Library of Congress Cataloging-in-Publication Data
Lancaster, John. 1930–
    Fabric Art / John Lancaster.
        p.   cm. — (Fresh start)
    Summary: Examines the crafts that can be made using different
yarns, threads, and fabrics.
    ISBN 0-531-14102-0
    1. Textile crafts—Juvenile literature.   2. Fiberwork—Juvenile
literature.   [1. Textile crafts.   2. Handicraft.]   I. Title.
TT699.L355   1991
746—dc20   90-12281
                                                            CIP AC

Design: K & Co
Editor: Jenny Wood
Typeset by Lineage
Printed in Belgium
The author would like to thank
the following people: Henry
Pluckrose for his editorial help
and advice during the preparation
of this book; Chris Fairclough for
his usual expertise with respect to
the photographic materials.

Contents

This book describes activities which use the following:

Bobbin (a wooden thread reel or a plastic bobbin)
Bowl (or basin, or similar container for mixing dyes)
Cane (an ordinary garden cane, length of basket cane or dowel rod)
Cardboard (used cardboard boxes and/or plain cardboard)
Craft knife
Darning needle (a large, blunt one)
Dyes — batik dyes
— cold water dyes
— fabric colors
— fabric crayons
— fabric paints
— fabric pens
— pastel colors
— pastel dye sticks
— textile dyes
(You could make a selection of two or three)
Fabric (remnants of a variety of solid and patterned dress fabrics)
Felt (scraps, white and various colors)
Glue
Iron (do not use the steam operation)

Jelly jar (or similar container)
Masking tape
Mixing stick (an old wooden kitchen spoon would do nicely)
Net curtain material (scraps, patterned white or colored)
Netting (plastic or nylon)
Newspaper
Paper (8½ x 11in typing paper or white drawing paper)
Paper towels
Pebbles (smooth, small and large)
Pen
Pencil
Plastic wastebasket liners
Plastic sheet (to cover your work surface)
Plate (old, or large cookie tin lid)
Raffia
Ribbon (a range of brightly colored lengths)
Rubber bands
Ruler (wooden, plastic or metal)
Saw
Scissors
String (thick, thin, smooth or rough)
Water
Wool (natural or "raw" sheep's wool and various colored yarns)

What is fabric?

Fabric is cloth that has been made either by hand or by machine. It is a material we use in many ways. Our clothes are made of fabric, and we have many fabric items in our homes – curtains, cushion covers, sheets, rugs, furniture coverings and towels are some examples.

Fabric is woven from either natural or synthetic (man-made) fibers. The fibers might be wool, cotton or nylon. Some are coarse and rough in texture, others are smooth and fine. Fabrics can be left in their natural colors, but it is also possible to color them with dyes and to pattern them in interesting ways.

In this book you will be shown some simple ways of making threads from natural wool. It is important to do this at the start so that you not only understand how fabric is made but also begin to appreciate the skills and materials used. You will go on to decorate some pieces of fabric in different ways, and you will be encouraged to experiment freely in developing ideas of your own. Have fun!

Some hints

Cover your work top (a table or a space on the floor) with a plastic sheet. Dyes can be messy and the plastic sheet will help you keep things clean and neat!

Wear an old shirt, apron or smock over your clothes. Remember to replace screw tops or lids on your fabric pens or tubes of ink immediately after use. Put all your materials away carefully after each working session. A large cardboard box is an ideal container. (You may prefer to have two – one for equipment, the other for pieces of fabric and other materials.)

1 A selection of different materials.

Weaving

Making a spindle

A spindle is a simple tool which is used to make a thread of wool. To make your own spindle you will need a length of cane or dowel rod between 10in and 12in long, a bobbin and a saw.

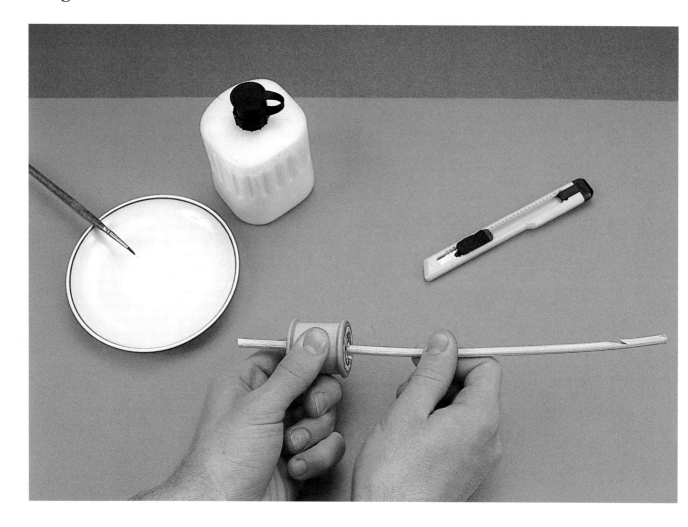

1 Insert the cane into the bobbin, leaving about 1in protruding from the base. (The base section is called a "whorl," and its purpose is to help the spindle spin.) Using the saw, carefully cut a small notch about 1in from the top end of the cane or "spindle stick" as it is now known.

Using your spindle to make a thread

You must now learn to make a woolen thread or "yarn." You will need a bundle of natural sheep's wool. (See page 39 for details of how to obtain this.)

2 Pull a small quantity of tangled fibers from the bundle. This is known as "teasing" and must be done firmly but gently.

3 Rub the fibers gently between your fingers to form a rough length of yarn.

Note: An experienced handweaver will normally use two wooden bats with small metal teeth (rather like hairbrushes) to form lengths of yarn. This process is known as "carding."

4 Tie your rough length of yarn to the spindle stick, then thread it through the notch at the top end. Spin the spindle carefully (not too fast) and you should begin to produce a length of twisted yarn which will collect around the spindle stick rather like a ball of wool.

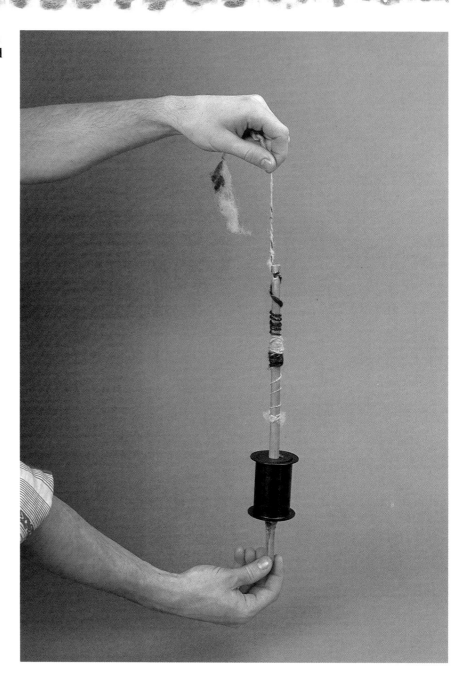

Take some more of the raw woolen fibers and repeat the whole process of teasing and carding, attaching your roughly-made yarn to the loose end of the yarn above the spindle stick.

Your woolen yarn will tend to be uneven. This does not matter – the important thing is that you have made some yarn and now know the process involved.

A reference chart

Now that you have made some yarn for yourself, collect a selection of samples of colored yarns.

5 Keep your samples in a box or folder, or arrange them on a sheet of cardboard. Stick them in place and write some notes underneath each to explain what it is – "Natural sheep's wool," "Natural spun threads" or "Colored wools bought locally," for example. A chart like this will be a useful reference for you.

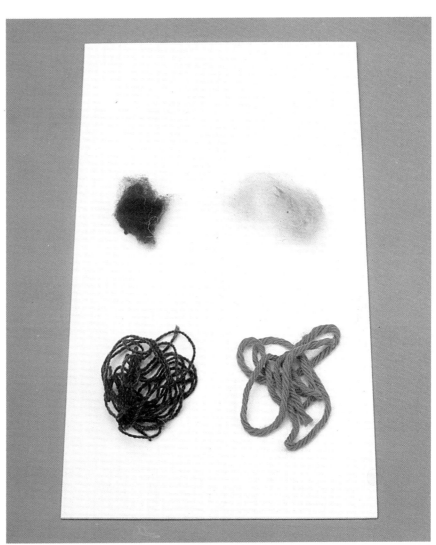

Fabric is made by a process called "weaving." In this process yarns are crossed over and under each other on a loom to form lengths of cloth. Some fabrics are loosely woven, others are tightly woven using cotton or silk threads. Some are coarse and heavily textured, others are fine and delicate.

Making a loom

A "cardboard loom" is easy to make. You will need a piece of cardboard, scissors, a pen or pencil, a ruler, and masking tape.

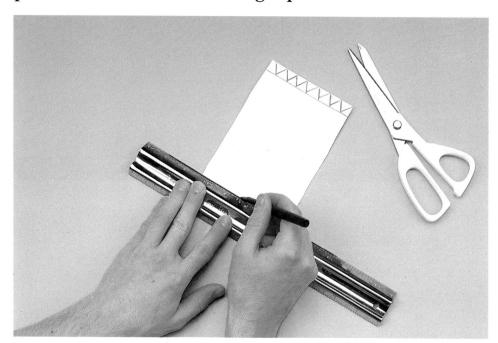

6 Cut a rectangle from the cardboard, approximately 7 x 5in (although your loom can be slightly smaller or larger). Draw a line about ¼in in from each of the shorter edges. Now draw a row of angled lines from the edges of the cardboard to the lines, as shown.

7 Cut along these angled lines to create a series of notches into which your "warp" will slot. The "warp" is a series of vertical threads on a loom, and is the basic framework of the woven fabric. The warp is made with a long length of yarn.

Use this formula to estimate how much yarn you will require to make a warp.

Count the notches across the cardboard.

Multiply the number of notches by the length of the cardboard loom.

Double the figure you have now reached, to allow for the fact that the yarn will have to be looped around the back of the loom.

(Note: The cardboard loom shown in picture **7** measures 7 x 5in, so the length of yarn needed to make the warp is estimated like this: **7** (notches) x **7in** (length of loom) x **2** (allowing for yarn around back of loom). **7 x 7 x 2 = 98in.** A few more inches were added to allow for securing loose ends at the back of the loom.)

8 Tape one end of the yarn behind the cardboard loom near to the bottom left-hand notch.

9 Wind the yarn firmly around the loom (from top to bottom of the cardboard), using the notches to position it. Tape down the other loose end and snip off any extra yarn.

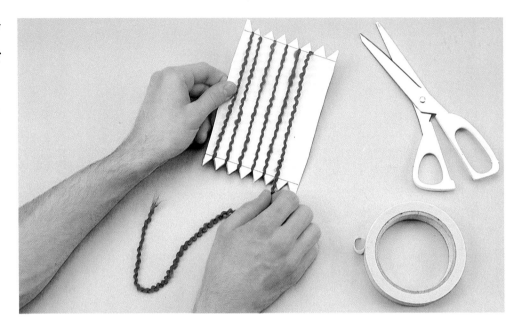

Weaving
You are now ready to start the weaving process. You need yarn in a different color, and a large, blunt darning needle.

10 To weave a piece of fabric, you need to make what is called the "weft." Using the darning needle, weave the second color of yarn from left to right then from right to left, under and over the "warp." Continue this process until you have produced a length of fabric.

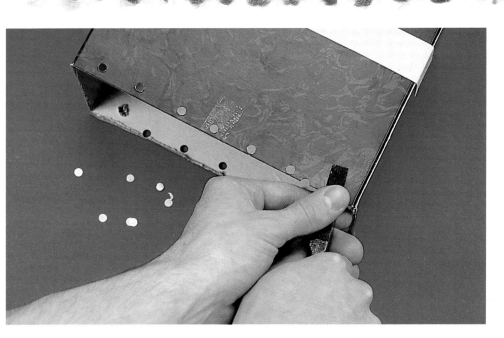

11 A cardboard box can be turned into another simple loom. Punch holes in two sides for the "warp" yarn.

12 Thread the "warp" yarn through the holes, then use another color to make the "weft," as before.

Tie-dye

A simple way of decorating some types of fabric is to use a method known as "Tie-Dye." You will need cold water dye, a jelly jar, water, a stick or old wooden spoon, an old basin or bowl, a piece of fabric (preferably cotton) approximately 12 x 12in, a pebble or smooth stone, strong rubber bands, an old plate or a pad of paper towels, and an iron.

Wear your apron, smock or old shirt when you are dyeing fabric, so that you do not splatter your clothes. Make sure your table is well covered, and try not to make too much of a mess!

1 Place some cold water dye in the jelly jar and add some water.

2 Mix well with the stick or old wooden spoon.

3 Pour the dye into the bowl.

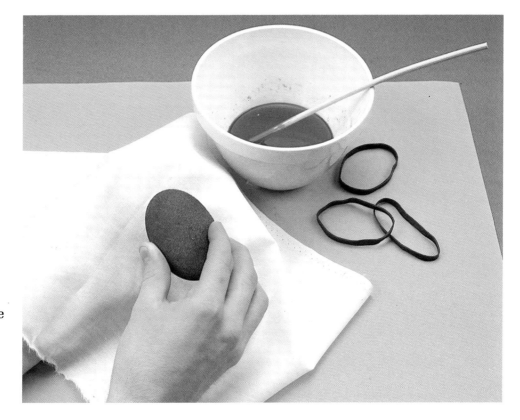

4 Place the pebble in the center of the fabric square. Hold the ends of the cloth together and twist the cloth around the pebble (with the pebble still inside!).

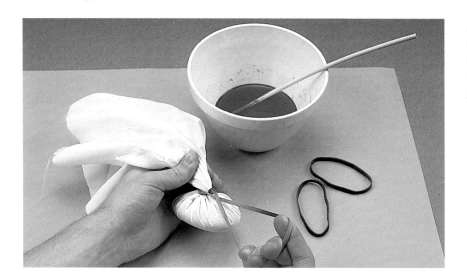

5 Now twist three or four strong rubber bands around and around the cloth as near to the pebble and as tightly as you can.

6 Take the end of the cloth and dip the "wrapped" pebble into the basin of dye.

7 Using the stick, press the cloth down under the dye and leave it to soak up some of the color. After two or three minutes lift the tied-up cloth and pebble out of the bowl and place on the plate or paper towels to dry.

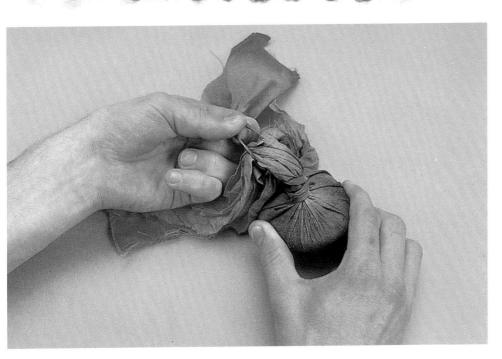

8 When dry, remove the rubber bands from the cloth and lift out the pebble.

9 The fabric square – now dyed with one color – will be patterned. The color will have taken in some places but not in others, especially the areas where the rubber bands were situated. Press your tie-dyed fabric square with a hot iron.

10 A selection of cotton and silk fabrics decorated using tiedye methods.

Other ideas

1 Why not try dyeing a piece of fabric more than once? After dipping it into a bowl of dye, allow it to dry. Now dip it again – either into the same color or into a different color. Allow it to dry then iron it.

2 Dip a piece of tied fabric once. Allow it to dry then add more rubber bands and dip it again into a different color of dye. This should give you an interesting two-color pattern.

3 Tie knots in a length of fabric, or tie string or raffia around it tightly in places then dye it. This time, however, instead of dipping the fabric into the dye, hold it above the bowl and apply dye to certain parts of the fabric with a brush. Do this with two or more colors.

4 Wrap some fabric around a short stick or dowel rod and twist rubber bands around it tightly. Dip the fabric into dye, leave to dry then iron flat.

It is now possible to buy a range of fabric printing dyes in the form of pens and crayons. These are easy to use and give effective results quickly. Fabric pens contain dye – in the form of an ink – and allow you to draw straight onto the cloth. Some crayons, too, may be used in this way, while with others you will need to draw your design on a piece of paper or cardboard first.

You will need fabric pens or crayons in different colors, pieces of fabric (white cotton is best), a pad of paper towels and an iron.

The way to fix these dyes permanently onto the fabric is to iron them with a hot, dry (not a steam) iron. The simple way to do this is shown in pictures 2, 3 and 4. However, it is absolutely essential to ask an adult for help with any ironing you might do.

1 Here a pattern has been drawn onto a square of white cotton fabric using brown, orange and blue fabric pens. Try drawing your own design straight onto a piece of fabric.

2 To fix the dye, place the patterned piece of fabric onto a pad of paper towels, newspaper or felt.

3 Lay a plain piece of fabric on top.

4 Using a sweeping movement, press the hot iron down onto the fabric then lift it off. Repeat this a number of times (for about two or three minutes), to ensure that the dye is fixed.

5 Interesting patterns and textures can be obtained by laying a piece of plastic netting over the cloth and stippling through the holes with a fabric pen.

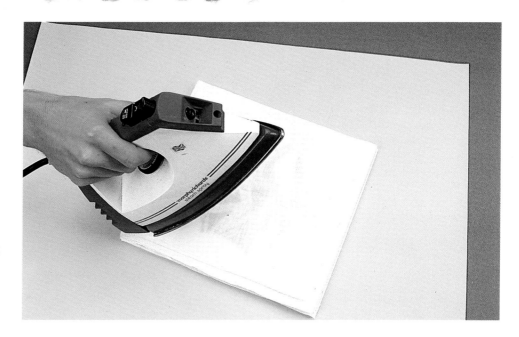

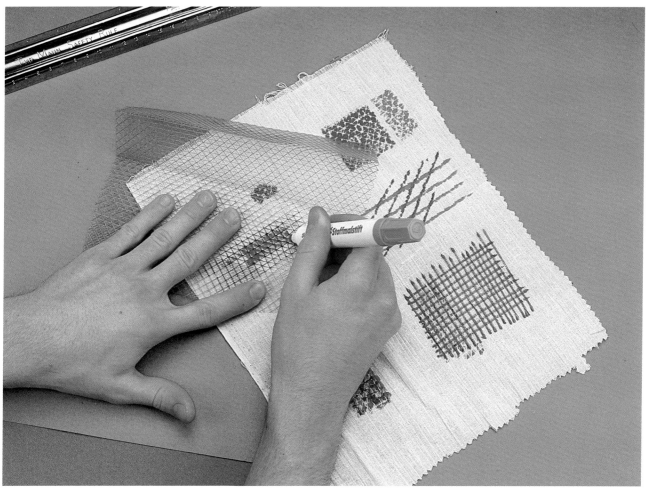

6 Here a fabric pen is being used to add blue dots to a pattern of crisscross lines. The fabric in the right of the picture shows three patterns which were created by first dampening parts of the fabric with a wet cloth, then applying color with fabric pens and pastel colors. Notice how the colors have spread and softened on the damp fabric. When the fabric had dried, patterns and shapes were drawn on top. Try this idea yourself.

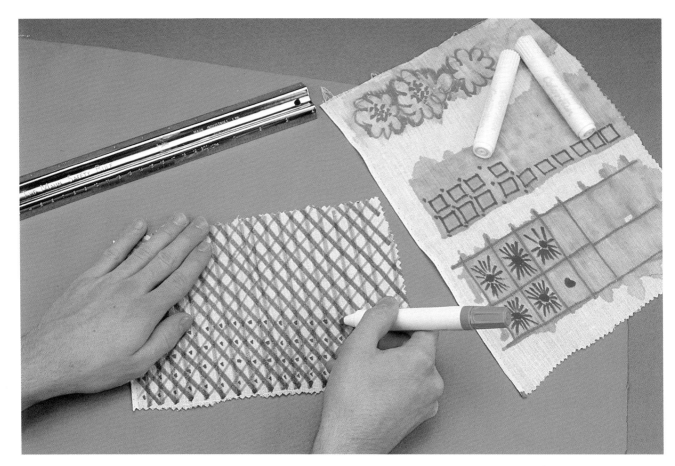

Useful "fixing" hints

1 When ironing, use a series of pressing and lifting motions: apply the iron and lift the iron/ apply the iron and lift the iron/ apply the iron and lift the iron until the whole design is covered.

2 Wash the decorated fabric gently in warm water.

3 Re-iron the fabric.

Drawing with pastel colors is easy. Use them carefully, however, for the pastel sticks tend to snap in two if you press down too hard.

You will need pastel sticks in different colors, white paper or cardboard, pieces of fabric (white cotton is best), paper towels and an iron.

1 Draw a pattern or picture on to a piece of white paper or cardboard. Press firmly but carefully.

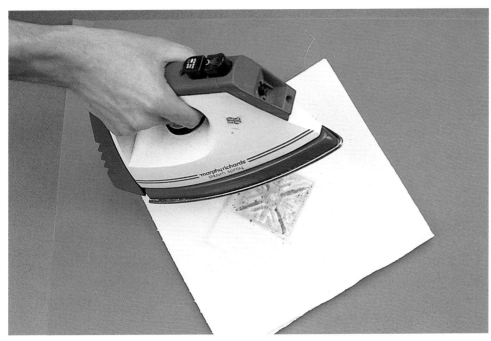

2 To transfer your design to fabric, place a piece of plain fabric on a pad of paper towels. Place your design face down on the fabric, and lay another piece of plain fabric on top. Iron firmly, using the method described on pages 19-21.

Pastel dye sticks are excellent for creating designs on plain fabric, silk scarves, tea towels, napkins and even T-shirts. You can draw directly onto the fabric. Follow the ironing method described on pages 19-21 to fix the colors.

You will need a selection of pastel dye colors in different colors, pieces of fabric, paper towels and an iron.

1 An idea for a design, based on squares.

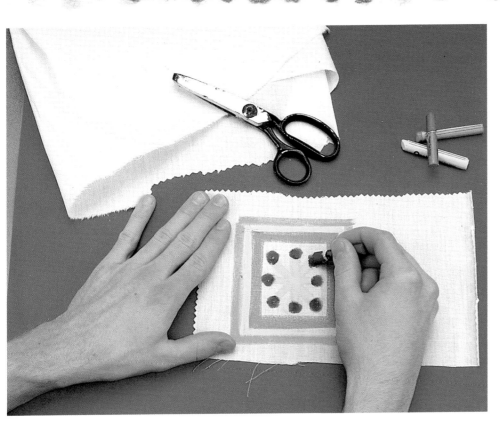

2 Make your design a little more elaborate by adding a series of dots.

3 Why not try a design of wavy lines?

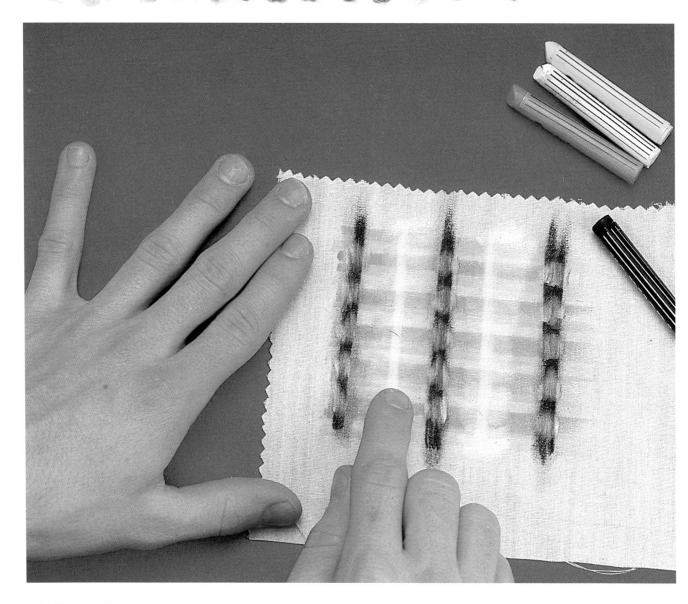

4 Rubbing white
crayon into a design
creates a softer effect.

This project is a fabric collage which combines three techniques: (1) creating a pattern on a piece of white felt using colored dyes; (2) building up a collage design with your patterned and plain pieces of felt; (3) adding colored pieces of net to give an "overlay" effect.

You will need a selection of textile dyes (fabric pens, pastel colors or pastel dye sticks in different colors), pieces of felt (white and colored), scissors, an old plate, water, glue, cardboard and pieces of net (in a variety of colors). Choose toning or contrasting colors for this project as you prefer.

1 Cut a piece of thin white felt approximately 8 x 6in. Place it on the plate and dampen it with a little cold water. Color the damp felt using lines, dots or other shapes, and take it off the plate to dry.

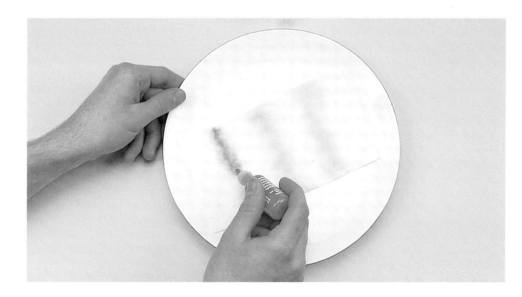

2 Glue a slightly larger piece of colored felt onto a rectangular piece of cardboard. This will act as the base on which you build up your collage. Spread some glue over one side of your patterned felt.

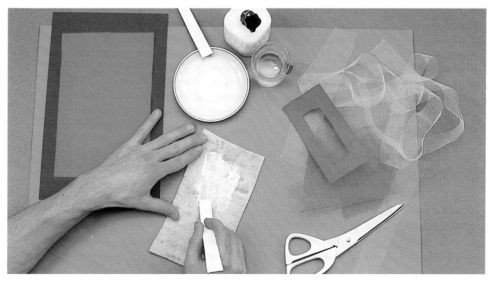

3 Position the patterned felt carefully on the colored felt base. Press it down firmly and allow the glue to dry.

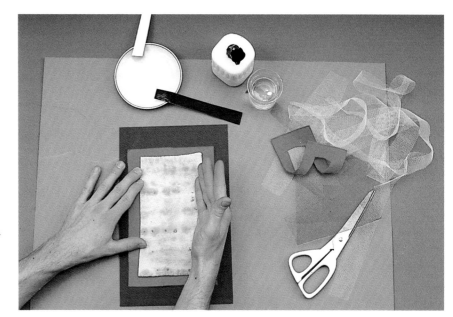

4 Add one or two more colored pieces of felt on top of the patterned piece. Now build up a net "overlay." Cut the net into various sizes and shapes. This, combined with the different colors, will create delicate, interesting effects.

Using brightly colored ribbons can be fun. The idea described here shows you how to make a row of mounted stripes.

You will need strong cardboard, scissors, lengths of ribbon (in a variety of colors), and masking tape or glue.

1 Cut a strip of strong cardboard (any size you like). Cut lengths of ribbon (long enough to go right around your strip of cardboard) in two or more colors. Tape or glue one end of each length of ribbon to the back of the cardboard strip.

2 Bring the other end of each length of ribbon right around the front of the cardboard and attach them on the back in the same way.

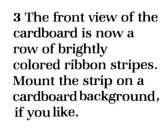

3 The front view of the cardboard is now a row of brightly colored ribbon stripes. Mount the strip on a cardboard background, if you like.

4 A different effect can be achieved by twisting each ribbon once or twice. Or you may prefer to attach only one end of each length of ribbon to the back of the cardboard strip, allowing the other end to hang free.

Experiment with ribbons and sticks (canes or dowel rods) to see what effects you can produce. Try incorporating colored ribbons into a piece of weaving. Try printing or drawing patterns on ribbons with your fabric pens and pastels.

Knotted threads can be used to make decorative hangings. You will need a selection of different colored lengths of woolen yarn, raffia or string, scissors, cardboard, and masking tape or glue.

1 Take a double thickness of yarn, raffia or string.

2 Tie a knot through the double thickness.

3 Pull the knot tight.

4 A selection of knots tied in yarns, string and raffia. Make a "Knot Sampler" by mounting some of your knots on cardboard and labeling them neatly.

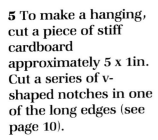

5 To make a hanging, cut a piece of stiff cardboard approximately 5 x 1in. Cut a series of v-shaped notches in one of the long edges (see page 10).

6 Place the loops in your lengths of knotted threads over the cardboard strip so that the threads drop into the notches. You might like to pull some of them tight. Tape or glue the threads to the back of the cardboard.

7 The long, dangling tails (or "fringes") can be left with unequal lengths or cut to the same length. Display your completed hanging from a ceiling hook or in front of a window.

8 Here the knotted yarns have been hung from a length of garden cane.

Other ideas
1 In order to vary the hanging, tie two or three knots in some of the lengths of thread.
2 Try tying two different colored threads together to create a thicker, richer texture.

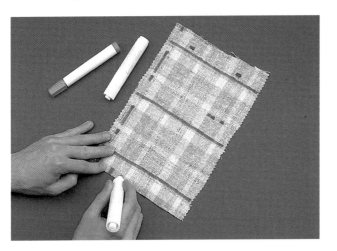

1 Plaid cloth or similar can be a helpful base on which to add colored squares, dots, circles or other shapes with fabric pens or crayons. Why not try doing something like this with other patterned textiles?

2 Make a collage from odd bits and pieces of cloth.

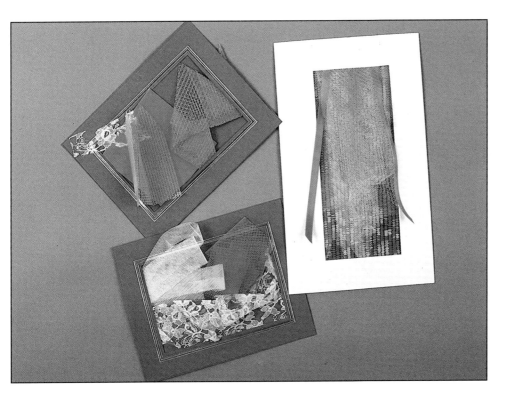

3 Attempt a different kind of collage using bits of felt, colorful oddments of dress material and pieces of net.

4 Exciting effects can be achieved by cutting and folding plain felt or cloth to reveal what is below. Try it!

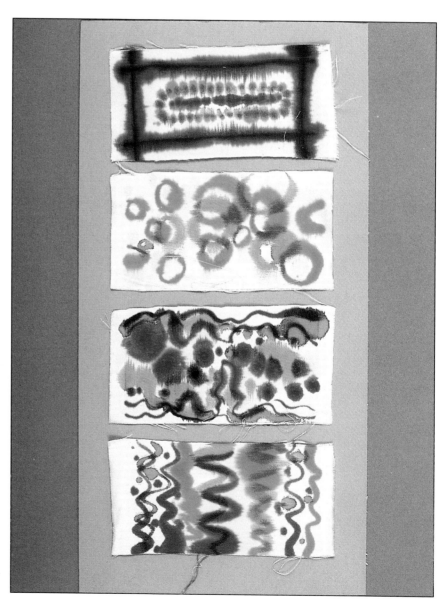

5 Tape some pieces of fabric to a board and color them in different ways. Be adventurous!

6 Look for unusual objects on which to weave. The experimental weaving shown here was done with wool, raffia and strips of plastic wastebasket liners using an old wire shelf as a simple loom. Look for other objects that could be used as a loom.

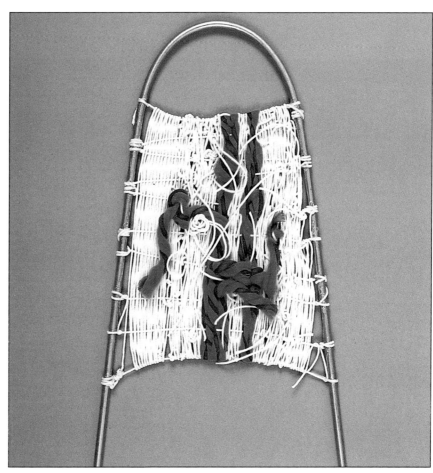

7 In this example a length of metal tubing has been bent, and a 'warp" and "weft" attached to it.

8 This decorative hanging shows how different textile materials may be combined. Experiment yourself by using twigs, straw, strips of newspaper, raffia, paper and other things.

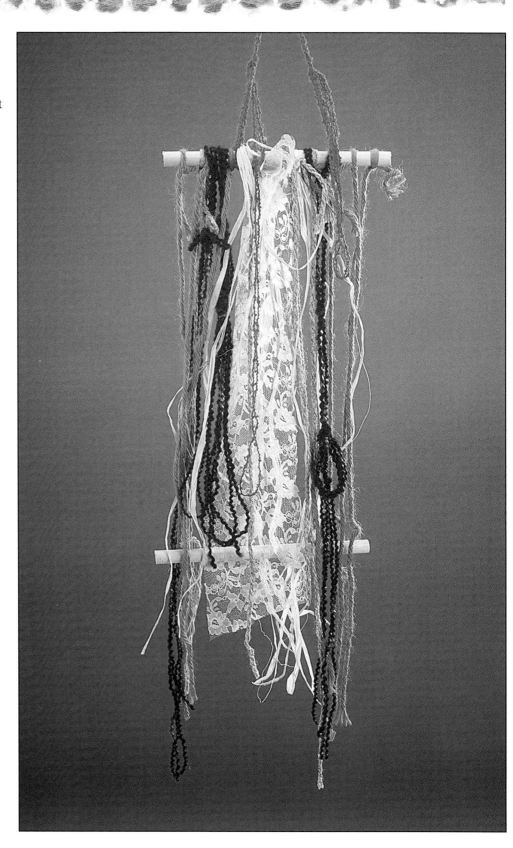

Stationery stores and/or art and crafts stores will stock many of the items of equipment listed in this book.

Basket cane may be bought in art and craft supply stores. Go to a garden center for garden canes.

Fabric
Seek remnants of plain cotton fabric, felt squares, patterned dress fabrics, net and nylon curtain materials etc., from sewing departments in large stores and from fabric stores.

Fabric dyes
There is a range of fabric dyes on the market and these are normally stocked by art and craft supply stores.
Crayola Fabric Colors can also be obtained through art and craft stores,
Deka Fluorescent Fabric Paints are useful for special effects.
Deka Series "L" Textile Dyes (Batik Colors) are mixed in boiling water. THEY REQUIRE ADULT SUPERVISION IF USED.

Batikit Cold Water Dyes are also recommended for use.
Pentel Fabric Fun Pastel Dye Sticks come in assorted boxes and are very good.
Niji, Dizzle and Vogart (Fabric Pens) are recommended.
(NOTE: ALL THESE FABRIC DYES COME WITH THEIR OWN INSTRUCTIONS. THESE SHOULD BE READ CAREFULLY AND FOLLOWED.)

Wool
Natural (raw) sheep's wool may be found in speciality craft supply stores.

Some helpful books
Collage by Hilary Devonshire (Franklin Watts)
Fun with Wool by Sylvia Pollard (Muller)
Applique (NC1), *Spindle Spinning* (**NC13**) **and** *Small Scale Weaving* (NC17) (The Search Press)